STARTING BALLET

Helen Edom, Nicola Katrak and Susan Meredith
(Nicola Katrak is a former principal dancer and artist in education with Birmingham Royal Ballet, England.)

Designed by Michèle Busby
Illustrated by Norman Young
Photographs by Bill Cooper and Angela Taylor

Additional photograph by Howard Allman

Contents

About ballet

Ballet is an exciting way of dancing which began hundreds of years ago. The movements of the dancers tell you a story or show you a mood. You can either go to see a ballet live on stage, or you can watch one on video.

A ballerina is a female dancer who dances leading parts in ballets.

Dancers make beautiful shapes with their bodies, arms and legs.

Ballet dancers make pointed shapes with their feet.

This kind of dress is called a tutu. It has a very short skirt so the dancer can move her legs easily.

This female dancer is dancing on pointe (see below).

The photographs in this book show dancers who have been training for years. If you start going to ballet classes, your teacher will encourage you to move to music and you will also do some of the simple exercises and steps shown in this book.

Female ballet dancers often dance on the very tips of their toes. This is called dancing on pointe (say point). It is very difficult to do, although dancers make it look easy.

Finding a class

To find a ballet class, you can look for advertisements in your local telephone directory, library or newspaper. (See also page 32.)

Ballet shoes

You can buy ballet shoes from dancewear shops. They have soft soles so you can point your feet. You can keep them on your feet with elastic.

What to wear

Wear clothes that are easy to move in, such as leggings or shorts. You must be able to point your toes, so it is best if you do your first ballet class in bare feet.

Tie your hair back out of the way.

Later on, if you like ballet, you can buy special clothes such as a leotard, tights, and ballet shoes. Ask your teacher before you decide what to buy.

Modern ballets

Dancers don't wear traditional costumes and shoes for all ballets. In modern ballets, you see different kinds of shapes and movements too.

The dancers in this modern ballet are pretending to be birds.

Dancers sometimes dance in bare feet.

3

Dancing shapes

Dancers use different shapes and movements to make a dance exciting to watch. See how many shapes you can make with your body. Stay still in each one for a few seconds.

A small, round shape.

What shape would your body make if you had to fit into a small box?

Strong arms help this shape to look fierce.

A wide, stretched shape.

How much room can you make your body take up if you really stretch?

This tall shape looks proud.

See how many shapes you can think of that make you look frightening or proud.

Shapes to spot

Here are some shapes ballet dancers often make. You may spot them when you see a performance.

Straight arm

Curved arm

Straight leg

Bent leg

This stretched shape is called an arabesque (say ara-besk).

This more rounded shape is called an attitude (say atty-tewd).

Ballet movements have French names because ballet steps were first written down in France, about 350 years ago.

4

Moving shapes

Try moving with a rounded back.

Your arms and legs tuck in when you roll.

You can stretch up as you skip or whirl.

Your legs stretch out as you slide.

Now try moving. How many different ways can you find to move across the room?

Starting from a rounded shape, try rolling, pouncing, crawling or creeping.

Then start from a stretched shape and try whirling, sliding, skipping or jumping.

Moving to music

Dragging steps could go with slow, sad music.

Energetic jumps might go with exciting music.

Hops and skips could go with cheerful music.

In ballet, as in most dancing, the movements are made to music. Listen to some music. How does it make you feel?

Think of ways you can move to suit the mood of the music. Remember to change your movements as the music changes mood.

Keeping in time

Dancers' movements often match the beat of the music. Listen to some music with a strong beat and clap or stamp in time.

Clap your hands against a friend's. Listen carefully to the music so you don't get faster and faster.

5

Making a good start

You might normally stand crookedly like this.

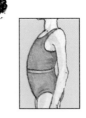

Look straight ahead.

Let your arms hang loosely by your sides.

Keep your back flat, not curved like this.

People often slouch when they stand. To dance well, you need to start from a good, straight position.

Dancers pull up their bodies so they are tall and straight. See if you can stand like a dancer.

Stand up tall with your feet together. Pull your tummy up to help you grow even taller.

Turning out

For ballet, you need to start with your legs turned out. Here are three different starting positions of the feet to try.

Your legs are turned out from the top.

Keep your body and legs well pulled up.

Your feet make a V-shape.

Stand firmly on both feet.

1. Bring both heels together and turn out your legs so that your toes point outward. This is called first position.

2. Put your feet a comfortable distance apart like this. Keep your legs turned out. This is called second position.

3. Put one heel halfway along the other foot. This is third position. You can do this with either foot in front.

Positions to spot

Feet are apart in fourth position.

Feet are together in fifth position.

After training to help them turn out their legs, ballet dancers are able to use two more foot positions (shown above). See if you can spot them when you watch ballet.

Lifting your legs

Ballet dancers move with their legs turned out. This helps them to lift their legs higher. Try this experiment to see how much difference turning out makes.

Arms turned in

Arms turned out

Put the backs of your hands on the sides of your legs. Without twisting your arms, see how high you can lift them up to each side.

Then, turn your arms out as they hang by your sides, so the palms are facing front. Now you can raise your arms as high as you like.

You can see how this dancer's legs are turned out from the top.

Keep your body upright.

Legs turned in

Legs turned out

Your legs work the same way but lifting them is harder.

Try with your feet straight, then with your feet turned out.

High lifts

Dancers train for years so their legs become strong and turned out enough to make shapes like this. A dancer needs to have very good balance too.

First movements

The first movements in a ballet class help to make your muscles warm and stretchy. You often start off with some leg bends.

Leg bends are called pliés (say plee-aze). When you first start ballet, you will probably do demi-pliés (half-bends).

Look straight ahead while you do this.

Don't stick your bottom out when you bend.

Keep both feet flat on the floor.

1. To do a demi-plié, start with your feet in a V-shaped first position. Stand up as tall as you can and put your hands on your waist.

2. Bend your knees slowly and smoothly so they go out over your toes. Then straighten your legs to stand tall again.

3. Now try a demi-plié starting with your feet apart in second position. Remember to go down and up very smoothly.

Using a barre

Dance rooms have a rail called a barre on the wall. You can hold this to help you balance. You rest your hands lightly on a barre but don't grip it. Your arms should be slightly bent.

If there is a mirror behind the barre, you can use it to check your position. Your teacher can help you do this.

This room has a double barre. You hold whichever one is comfortable for your height.

Trying at home

Your barre should be about waist-height.

You can use the back of a steady chair or a table instead of a barre when you do ballet at home.

Body bends

Try another bending movement, this time for your back.

Your back curves as it bends.

Your arms hang loosely by your sides.

Keep your knees straight.

1. Stand up tall with your feet in first position. Let your head feel heavy, and slowly and gently drop it forward.

2. Gently bend your whole body forward, following your head. Let your arms flop down toward the floor.

Some people can bend far enough to touch the floor.

Keep your feet flat on the floor in first position.

3. Bend over only as far as feels comfortable. The more times you do this, the easier it will be to bend.

4. Straighten up slowly and smoothly so your head comes up last of all. Keep your legs tall and straight all the time.

Ballet training

Professional dancers go to classes every day to make their muscles supple and strong. They always begin with pliés.

A demi-plié in fifth position.

Dancers do pliés in all five foot positions (see page 6). First they do a demi-plié, then they go down into a grand plié (say gron plee-ay). Grand plié means big bend.

The arm movements change along with the legs.

A grand plié in fifth position.

Moving your arms

In ballet, the way you move your arms is just as important as the way you move your legs. You often make round or softly curved shapes like these.

A dancer keeps her arms soft, even when she makes a strong movement with her legs.

Shapes and movements

Let your fingers curve as well as your arms.

Try not to hunch your shoulders.

Let your eyes follow your hands as you move them.

Your arms are still gently curved.

1. Stand up tall with your arms by your sides. Then lift your arms up smoothly in front of you to make a circle in front of your tummy. This is called first position.

2. Keep your arms in the circle shape and raise them smoothly until they are almost above your head. Keep your shoulders down. This is called fifth position.

3. Open your arms out as if you were drawing a curve on each side of you. This is called second position. To finish, lower your arms back to your sides again.

Arm waves

Gently press the air away
with the back of your hand
as your arm goes up.

Try this
kneeling or
standing.

Push the air away
with your palm
as your arm
comes down.

See if you can make
your arms move
like birds' wings.
Wave them up and
down as smoothly
as if you were
underwater.

Mixed positions

You can swap your
arms and try these
positions the other
way around.

You can hold one
arm in first position
and the other arm
in second. This
mixture is called
third position.

Fourth position is
another mixture.
You hold one arm
in fifth position and
the other arm in
second position.

Wings

Dancers sometimes
move their arms to
make them look like
wings and beaks.
The dancers in
these photographs
are pretending to
be swans.

The dancer
stretches
his arms
behind him
like wings.

He makes his
hands look
like a beak.

The dancers
fold their
arms over
their heads
like wings.

11

Pointing your feet

Ballet dancers point their feet so that they make a long, graceful line with their legs. Try these exercises to help you get used to pointing your feet whenever you do ballet.

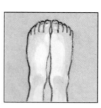

Keep your feet and ankles in a straight line.

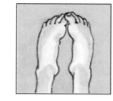

Don't let your feet curve into a banana shape.

Even when dancers are doing big jumps, they still point their feet.

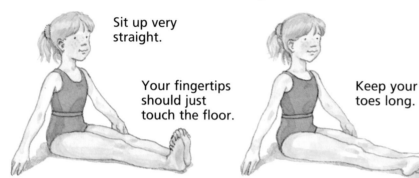

Sit up very straight.

Your fingertips should just touch the floor.

Keep your toes long.

1. Sit on the floor with your legs straight in front of you. Bend your ankles so your toes point up to the ceiling.

2. Slowly stretch your toes as far down to the ground as you can. The more you do this, the easier it becomes.

This jump is called a fish step because the dancer's body looks rather like a leaping fish.

Trotting with pointed feet

Lift up your heel before your toes.

Point your toes as you lift them.

On the way down your toes should touch the ground first.

As you get faster you can lift your feet higher.

See if you can point your toes while you lift up one foot at a time.

Start by standing up tall with your feet together. Go slowly at first.

As you get good at this, go faster so you look like a pony trotting on the spot.

12

Quiet movements

Your movements become lighter and quieter when you point your feet. See how quietly you can skip with your toes pointed.

You could use your quiet, pointed toes to pretend to creep into a secret place.

Try marching or walking with pointed feet to see how lightly you can move.

Swing your arms as you walk.

Sliding and pointing

Dancers strengthen their feet with movements called battements tendus (say bat-mon-ton-doos). They slide their feet to the front, side or back. This is how to do a battement tendu to the front.

Pull your body up as tall as you can.

Your feet make a V-shape in first position.

1. Stand up tall with your feet in first position. Put your hands on your waist or hold onto a barre.

Both legs are straight all the time.

Keep both legs turned out all the time.

2. Slide one foot forward firmly as if it is polishing the floor and start to point your toes.

Imagine that your toes are making a tiny toeprint, not a big splotch.

Your toes never leave the ground.

3. Hold your toes pointed while you count to three. Then slide your foot back to first position.

This dancer is doing a battement tendu to the side.

13

Rising and balancing

Once you can stand up tall like a dancer
(see page 6), you can learn to rise up on
your toes and balance. In ballet, this is
called standing on demi-pointe, or half-toe.

Pulling up

It's easier to
balance if you
look straight
ahead.

Start with your feet
together, making yourself
as tall as you can. Make
your legs long and
stretched too. Then try to
grow even taller. Breathe in
and rise up on your toes.

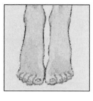 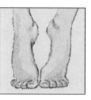

Keep all your
toes firmly on
the ground
like this.

Don't let your
feet curve into
a banana shape
like this.

Slowly lower your heels to
the ground again, breathing
out. Still keep your body
and legs as tall as you can.

Now try rising up with
your feet in first position.
Remember to come down
with your feet in the V-shape.

First position
on demi-
pointe.

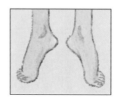

Dancing on pointe

It takes
several years
of training before
a girl's feet and legs
are strong enough
for her even to start
work on full pointe.

Dancing
on pointe
is hard
but has to
look easy.

If you go on pointe
before you are about 11, you will
damage your feet because the bones
in your toes are still soft at the ends.

Pointe shoes

Dancers wear shoes with strong soles
to go on pointe. The satin around
the toes is stiffened with glue but
there is no block inside.

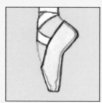

Pointe shoes
are tied on
with ribbons.

Pointe shoes have
to fit perfectly. The
toes are kept long
inside them, not
curled over.

Balancing on one leg

You can try balancing on one leg to make a shape called a retiré (say ret-ear-ay).

Keep your body straight to help you balance.

One foot stays flat on the floor.

Rest your hands lightly on your barre.

Your knee should be out to the side all the time.

Keep your foot pointed.

How long can you balance in this position?

Your toes fit into a hollow at the front of your knee.

1. Stand tall in first position. Point one foot and put the toes on your other ankle.

2. Slide your toes smoothly up the side of your leg. Keep both legs turned out.

3. Stop still when your toes are by your knee. Now let go of your barre.

Balancing on pointe

A balance on pointe.

A retiré position on demi-pointe.

Male dancers balance on demi-pointe but you hardly ever see them on full pointe.

Female ballet dancers learn to balance on one leg while they are on pointe.

Test your balance

Make any shape that helps you balance.

Dancers need good balance. Try to stand on one foot on demi-pointe. Can you stay still without wobbling?

15

Stretching your legs

Ballet dancers move their legs lightly and smoothly. They stretch them out straight, even when they are lifting them in the air.

Stretch your legs and point your toes when you try out these movements. You can hold onto a barre if you like.

Push your foot quickly and strongly so you hear a swishing noise.

Your toes point as you slide them out.

Your toes are only just above the ground.

Keep both knees straight all the time.

1. This battement glissé (say bat-mon-glee-say) starts like a tendu (see page 13) to the side. From first position, slide one foot out sideways.

2. As soon as your toes are fully pointed, stretch your leg even more so your toes just leave the floor. Keep your body pulled up straight.

3. Lower your pointed toes and slide your foot back to first position. Dancers do this very fast, and to the front and back as well.

Going higher

Try to keep your body still.

Keep your legs straight.

You can lean forward slightly when you throw your leg behind.

This dancer is throwing his leg up to the front in a grand battement.

Now try throwing your leg higher after sliding it out. Then lower it smoothly back to the floor.

This movement is called a grand battement. You can do this to the front and back as well as to the side.

16

Gallop steps

This is easier to do than it looks.

This boy is moving from left to right.

Swing your leg out.

Hop off this leg.

Point your toes.

Stretch your legs as much as you can.

Bend your left leg as you land.

Strong, stretched legs will help you to make bouncy gallop steps. Start by swinging your right leg to the side, then step onto it.

Hop up from your right foot and close your legs in midair. Land on your left foot and swing your right leg out again.

Keep going, bouncing as high as you can with each step. Then try going the other way by swinging out your left leg first.

Arabesques

Keep your eyes still to help you balance.

Stretch this arm out low to the side.

Your front arm is stretched out in front of your nose.

There is a long line from front finger to back toe.

An arabesque with the arms this way around is called a second arabesque.

Dancers do arabesques (see page 4) with their arms in different positions. The arabesque above is called a first arabesque. See if you can copy it.

An arabesque with both arms in front is called a third arabesque.

17

Jumping

Whenever you jump, you have to bend your legs before you can spring up. See how high you go if you crouch down and spring up like a frog. You could also try pouncing like a cat. How far can you travel through the air?

Your legs are very bent like this.

Straighten your legs a little as you spring up.

Pouncing like a cat.

Jumping from a demi-plié

Keep your body straight and tall.

Demi-plié

First position

Point your feet and straighten your legs.

Land as softly as you can.

Open your legs in midair to land in second position.

Don't stick your bottom out when you land.

Second position

When you jump in ballet, you keep your back straight as you bend your legs. Start by standing in first position.

Bend into a demi-plié, then jump up, straightening your legs and pointing your feet. Land in a quiet demi-plié.

This sort of jump is called a sauté (say so-tay). Now start a sauté in first position and land in second position.

Jumping on one leg

In some ballet steps, you jump from one foot to the other. Stand on one leg and put your other foot behind your calf. Then spring up and swap over so you land on the other leg. How many times can you do this?

This type of jump is called a petit jeté (say pet-ee-je-tay).

Your toes are just behind your calf.

Bend your leg as you land on it.

18

Flying jumps

Ballet training makes dancers' legs strong and supple. This helps them to jump very high in the air.

Dancers do flying jumps like these at the end of a class. Their muscles have to be very warm so they don't hurt themselves.

Looking up helps to make a jump look higher.

Dancers can stretch both legs out at the same time like this.

The dancers point their toes in the air.

Grand jeté

Try a flying jump called a grand jeté (say gron-je-tay). This means a big leap. You need lots of space.

Try to make stretched arm shapes.

Stretch out your legs while they are in the air.

Look up as you jump.

Do this when you are warm.

Run with your legs and arms stretched out to help you take long strides. Make one stride into a jump by taking off from one foot and landing on the other.

Always bend your leg as you land.

19

Turning

Ballet dancers spin and whirl in many exciting ways, both on the ground and in the air.

This dancer is doing a turn on the ground.

This is a turn on demi-pointe. Female dancers also spin on pointe.

Around in one go

See if you can jump like this and turn around in the air before you land.

The higher you jump, the further you can turn.

Keep your legs together and point your toes.

Some dancers jump so high they can turn two or even three times while in the air.

Turning in the air

Demi-plié in first position.

Bend your knees in a demi-plié as you land.

Turning in the air is easier if you start by jumping only a quarter of the way around at a time. From a demi-plié in first position, jump up, pointing your toes.

Turn a quarter in the air so you land in first position facing to the side. Do more quarter-turns so that you face the back, the other side, then the front again.

When you can do this, see if you can jump halfway, and then all the way around in one jump. These turns are called tours en l'air (say toor-on-lair).

Spinning and twirling

Use your arms to help you get around.

You can move your feet in tiny steps or twirl on one leg.

How many ways can you find to turn quickly without jumping? If you spin for long, you get dizzy. Ballet dancers have a trick so that they don't get dizzy (see below).

The spotting trick

Dancers keep looking at the same spot as they turn. This stops them from getting dizzy.

Try this trick slowly at first, then get faster and faster. Look at a spot straight ahead. Keep looking at it while you do tiny steps to make a slow turn.

When you can no longer keep your eyes on your spot, whip your head around quickly to find it again. Keep turning until your body is facing the front again.

Pirouettes

In ballet, a spin around on one leg is called a pirouette (say pir-oo-et).

This dancer is using the spotting trick. His body is facing the side, but he is looking to the front.

Holding his arms out like this helps him to balance.

This leg has to be straight.

He puts the toes of one foot by his other knee.

Dancers can do lots of fast pirouettes without stopping.

21

Dancing together

You can try out some of the ballet shapes and movements you have learned with your friends. See how good they look when people do them together as a team.

Watch the person in front so you move at the same time.

These dancers are all doing the same attitude position.

How many floor patterns can you make with your friends? Try standing in a straight line or making a triangle or circle shape.

A triangle shape

The corps de ballet

In many ballets, groups of people dance exactly the same movements together and make patterns on the floor. These groups of people are called the corps de ballet (say cor-de-balay).

It takes a lot of practice for the dancers to move exactly in time with one another.

This photograph shows members of a corps de ballet as swans in the ballet, Swan Lake.

Dancing in pairs

Stand facing your friend.

It's easier to balance on one leg if you hold onto a partner.

Ask a friend to do her own slow movements. Copy her exactly as if you are her reflection in the mirror.

Can you do a petit jeté (see page 18) at exactly the same time as your friend? How many can you do?

Instead of copying each other's movements, you could help each other to balance in interesting shapes.

Pas de deux

In ballet, a man and a woman often dance in a pair. This is called a pas de deux (say pa-de-de).

The man may lift the woman high into the air.

The dancers have to make a pas de deux look effortless.

The man helps the woman to balance.

The men do weight training to build up their strength.

23

Characters

Dancers play many different characters in ballet stories. Since they don't speak, their movements must show what sort of people they are.

See if you can turn yourself into a different person. You could be a rich prince, a wicked wizard or a fierce animal. Or you could be someone who is funny, happy, cold or angry.

How can a wizard make a jump look evil?

What shape might an old person make with her back?

Think how a spy might move his feet when he walks.

Find a way of moving for your character, then freeze in a still shape. What would your character do with her hands, head and body?

Try this with other characters. Think of different ways of moving for each one.

Think of ways to prowl like a lion.

Costumes in ballet

Dancers' clothes give clues to show what characters they are playing.

Dancers often wear floating white dresses with wings to show that they are spirits.

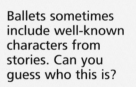

Ballets sometimes include well-known characters from stories. Can you guess who this is?

The decoration on this lady's clothes and the rich-looking fabric show that she is grand and wealthy.

Dressing up

Wrap tinsel around a hairband to make a princess's crown.

Dance with a ribbon tied around your wrist.

You can make swirling movements with a cloak.

Use face paints to give yourself a clown's face.

You could find costumes to help you show different characters. They must be easy to move in.

Use dark cloth for a witch's cloak. You could stick on stars and moons cut out of shiny paper.

A funny character could wear clothes that are much too big. Ask if you can sew or glue on patches.

Masks

Sometimes dancers wear masks to show their characters. They have to be specially made so they are light enough to dance in and so the dancer can see out.

These masks help the dancers to look like cats in the ballet, The Sleeping Beauty.

Animals

This dancer has to be careful not to trip over his tail.

Sometimes dancers have to wear not just a mask, but a full headpiece and costume which transform them completely. These can be heavy, hot and uncomfortable to dance in.

One of the Two Bad Mice in the ballet, Tales of Beatrix Potter.

Without words

In ballet, dancers don't speak but they can use signs to help to tell a story. Using signs instead of words is called mime. It is easy to guess what some mime means. Pointing to an eye means "see", pointing to an ear means "hear", pointing to the heart means "like" or "love".

Here is some other mime you may see in a ballet.

Afraid

Married (pointing to her ring finger)

Why?

Read

Please

Thanking

You can use this sign to thank your teacher after a class or an audience after a performance. It is called a révérence (say rev-air-ronce).

Hold out your hand to the person you are thanking and drop your head for a few seconds.

Girls may also take one leg behind the other and bend both knees in a curtsy.

Bow your head as you bend your knees.

Mime puzzle

You can make up sentences with mime signs. Can you tell what this girl is trying to say? (The answer is on page 32.)

26

Parties in ballets

Parties are a good excuse for lots of people to dance together. You can see parties and grand balls in many ballets.

This photograph shows children dancing together at a Christmas party in a ballet called The Nutcracker.

Pretend party

You could make up a party scene with your friends. Instead of talking, use the mime signs on page 26 and make up some other signs of your own. This is even more fun to music. Try making up happy dance steps to show that everyone is having a good time.

Smile and wave to say "hello".

Your hands show how big your present is.

Show how carefully you can pour a drink.

Putting on a performance

Lots of different people work together to put on a ballet performance. Together they are called a ballet company.

Making up a ballet

Marks show the position of the dancers' legs and arms.

A choreographer chooses the music for a new ballet and makes the movements to go with it. These can be written down in signs like this.

Designing the ballet

A designer thinks up ideas for scenery. A model stage shows how the scenery will look. A lighting designer tries out different ways of lighting the stage on the model.

Then, artists paint the full-size scenery onto huge sheets of canvas. Rocks and other objects are made of polystyrene, papier-mâché, or a special kind of foam.

Costumes

A designer draws ideas for the costumes. A wardrobe team makes the costumes so they look like the drawings.

Rehearsals

The dancers rehearse, or repeat, the steps many times to music. A few days before the performance, they begin to rehearse in the costumes on the stage. These are called dress rehearsals.

A dancer gets used to dancing in a tutu at rehearsals.

Thick tights and a top help the dancer to keep warm.

Make-up

All the dancers wear thick make-up so their faces show up under the bright stage lights. They put this on just before a dress rehearsal or a performance.

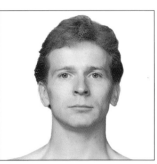

Before make-up

During make-up

With make-up complete

The performance

Dancing, music, costumes and scenery all help the audience to enjoy a performance. This photograph shows the last scene of the ballet, The Sleeping Beauty. The prince and the princess are in the middle.

They have been celebrating their wedding at the palace. The two people standing near the front are the king and queen, the princess's parents. Fairies perch high up on the scenery at the back.

Famous ballets

Ballets often tell magical stories, like fairy tales. Here are photographs from just a few of the ballets you might enjoy seeing.

The Nutcracker

Clara with the nutcracker

A little girl called Clara is given a doll-shaped nutcracker at Christmas. The nutcracker turns into a soldier prince, who takes Clara on a magical journey.

Coppélia

A toymaker thinks that one of his dolls (Coppélia) has come to life. But it is really only one of the village girls who has dressed up in the doll's clothes to trick him.

Peter and the Wolf

In this ballet, a boy, Peter, and his animal friends outwit a wolf. Dancers play the parts of trees in a forest and ripples on a pond as well as animals.

The cat

The bird

Trees in a forest

The wolf

A ripple on a pond

The Sleeping Beauty

A wicked fairy cast a spell that the princess would die. Here, a good fairy (in the middle) has put her and the court to sleep instead. She will be woken by a prince's kiss.

The flying fairies in this photograph are really hanging on wires that you cannot see. They are fastened to the wires by harnesses which they wear under their costumes.

Cinderella

In Cinderella, the parts of Cinderella's ugly sisters are usually danced by men.

Tales of Beatrix Potter

In this ballet, dancers bring to life some of the animal characters from Beatrix Potter's books.

This character is called Jemima Puddle-duck.

Index

Answer to the mime puzzle on page 26:
"Please, you, be quiet!"

Finding out more

You can write to these addresses to help you find a good ballet class.

Royal Academy of Dancing,
36 Battersea Square,
London, SW11 3RA, **UK**.

Royal Academy of Dancing,
15 Franklin Place,
Rutherford, NJ 07070, **USA**.

Royal Academy of Dancing,
20 Farrel Avenue,
Darlinghurst, NSW 2010,
Australia.

Royal Academy of Dancing,
404/3284 Younge Street,
Toronto, Ontario, M4N 2L6,
Canada.

Royal Academy of Dancing,
Walsh Wrightson Towers,
Level 2/94 Dixon Street,
PO Box 11718, Wellington,
New Zealand.

School visits

Many ballet companies hold workshops in schools. Try asking your teacher to find out if a ballet company can visit your school.

The photographs in this book are reproduced by courtesy of Bill Cooper: front cover, 1, 2, 3 (bottom right), 4, 6, 7, 9, 10, 11, 12, 13, 14, 15, 16, 17 (bottom right), 19, 20, 21, 22, 23, 24, 25 (bottom left), 26, 27, 28, 29 (top), 30 (top left), 31; Angela Taylor: back cover, 8, 17 (bottom left), 25 (bottom right), 29 (bottom), 30 (top right and bottom); Howard Allman: 3 (top right). With thanks to The Imperial Society of Teachers of Dancing, whose pupils are shown in the photographs on the back cover and on page 8.